Revelation

REVELATION

an apocalypse in fifty-eight fights

prose poems by

Andrew Rihn

Press 53
Winston-Salem

Press 53, LLC
PO Box 30314
Winston-Salem, NC 27130

First Edition

IMMERSION POETRY SERIES
edited by Christopher Forrest

Copyright © 2020 by Andrew Rihn

All rights reserved, including the right of reproduction
in whole or in part in any form except in the case of brief
quotations embodied in critical articles or reviews.
For permission, contact publisher at
editor@Press53.com, or at the address above.

Cover Art, "Classic Vintage Boxing Ring,"
© 2015 by allanswart. Licensed through iStock.

Excerpt(s) from THE SATANIC VERSES by Salman Rushdie,
copyright © 1988 by Salman Rushdie. Used by permission of Viking
Books, an imprint of Penguin Publishing Group, a division of
Penguin Random House LLC. All Rights Reserved.

Cover design by Christopher Forrest & Kevin Morgan Watson

Library of Congress Control Number
2019951122

Printed on acid-free paper
ISBN 978-1-950413-16-4

for all the long shots

Many thanks to the editors of the following journals, where versions of these poems first appeared:

Atlas and Alice, "Tyson vs. Alderson," "Tyson vs. Richardson" & "Tyson vs. Young"

Barren Magazine, "Tyson vs. Johnson," "Tyson vs. Berbick," "Tyson vs. Smith" & "Tyson vs. McNeeley"

Connotation Press, "Tyson vs. Tillis," "Tyson vs. Gross," "Tyson vs. Hosea" & "Tyson vs. Boyd"

DIAGRAM, "Tyson vs. Benjamin," "Tyson vs. Zouski," "Tyson vs. Green" & "Tyson vs. Ribalta"

Digging Press, "Tyson vs. Francis," "Tyson vs. Savarese" & "Tyson vs. Golota"

Five:2:One, "Tyson vs. Mercedes" & "Tyson vs. Halpin"

Horseshoes and Hand Grenades, "Tyson vs. Sims"

The Hunger, "Tyson vs. Canady," "Tyson vs. Long," "Tyson vs. Scaff" & "Tyson vs. Ferguson"

Into the Void, "Tyson vs. Frazier," "Tyson vs. Thomas" & "Tyson vs. Botha"

Miracle Monocle, "Tyson vs. Spain," "Tyson vs. Nelson" & "Tyson vs. Jaco"

Contents

Foreword by Christopher Forrest, Editor	xi
Tyson vs. Mercedes	3
Tyson vs. Singleton	4
Tyson vs. Halpin	5
Tyson vs. Spain	6
Tyson vs. Alderson	7
Tyson vs. Sims	8
Tyson vs. Canady	9
Tyson vs. Johnson	10
Tyson vs. Long	11
Tyson vs. Colay	12
Tyson vs. Benjamin	13
Tyson vs. Richardson	14
Tyson vs. Nelson	15
Tyson vs. Scaff	16
Tyson vs. Young	17
Tyson vs. Jaco	18
Tyson vs. Jameson	19
Tyson vs. Ferguson	20
Tyson vs. Zouski	21
Tyson vs. Tillis	22
Tyson vs. Green	23
Tyson vs. Gross	24
Tyson vs. Hosea	25
Tyson vs. Boyd	26
Tyson vs. Frazier	27
Tyson vs. Ribalta	28
Tyson vs. Ratliff	29
Tyson vs. Berbick	30
Tyson vs. Smith	31
Tyson vs. Thomas	32
Tyson vs. Tucker	33
Tyson vs. Biggs	34
Tyson vs. Holmes	35
Tyson vs. Tubbs	36
Tyson vs. Spinks	37

Tyson vs. Bruno I	38
Tyson vs. Williams	39
Tyson vs. Douglas	40
Tyson vs. Tillman	41
Tyson vs. Stewart	42
Tyson vs. Ruddock I	43
Tyson vs. Ruddock II	44
Tyson vs. McNeeley	45
Tyson vs. Mathis Jr.	46
Tyson vs. Bruno II	47
Tyson vs. Seldon	48
Tyson vs. Holyfield I	49
Tyson vs. Holyfield II	50
Tyson vs. Botha	51
Tyson vs. Norris	52
Tyson vs. Francis	53
Tyson vs. Savarese	54
Tyson vs. Golota	55
Tyson vs. Nielson	56
Tyson vs. Lewis	57
Tyson vs. Etienne	58
Tyson vs. Williams	59
Tyson vs. McBride	60
Notes	63
About the Author	81

Foreword

What does the man aspiring to open a curiosity shop say first? *I need to get my hands on some peculiar skeletons and mysterious weaponry.* Maybe. *How much must I budget for one of those machines that stamps pennies into oval tokens?* Very possibly. It could be, though, he simply opens his doors—he, himself, curious—and waits for what might arrive.

And so I've introduced my grand metaphor for the Immersion Poetry Series. This curiosity shop, craving inventory, beckons readers to walk in and ask, *How might I like to engage humanity today? With what conduit can I sympathize? Whom and what can I assume?*

There isn't a checklist and I'm not waiting on the poetry equivalent of novelty shot glasses, treasure maps, or conjoined twin gerbil skeletons. The subject matter is as much a mystery to me as it is to you. The Immersion Poetry Series could be a home for books on how pianos are made, viruses, life as a first responder, the Mercator projection, or competitive dog grooming, as long as it allows the reader a lens to reframe their own perspective and circumstance, to learn something, to sink themselves into an unfamiliar world, and resurface glad they did.

In the end, the books aren't only about their subjects, but how you engage them: how you understand our community and say, *Look at this world, look at what this human—exactly what I am—pays attention to. What does that mean to me?*

This is a home for exceptional poets not to temper but to celebrate and probe their passions. And it is a place for readers to vacation, and, like any good one, try to bring a bit of it home with them.

I am proud to present Andrew Rihn's debut book-length collection and the first book of poems in the Immersion

Poetry Series, *Revelation: An Apocalypse in Fifty-Eight Fights*, immersing us into the bouts of Mike Tyson. Layered into these fights is an apologue for the biblical Elijah, a man-at-arms against the world. Rihn transcends the inherent controversy of Tyson-based subject matter by offering not an apology, not redemption, not flattery nor ignorance, but a trenchant examination of our greatest observable cycle, the only one that really matters: the beginning and the end.

The relationship between boxing and poetry is a ubiquitous one. (The puns, my God, the puns.) Boxing is *poetry in motion*. It's the *sweet science of bruising*. The love they both command feels classic, nostalgic. There is appreciation independent of understanding. If poetry is a supreme application of language, boxing could be our physical being at its most supreme utility. If our brains are programmed for gestalt hemispheric response to metered verse, in the same way master musicians use the "left" and "right" brains in tandem, in the same way the human brain can respond to LSD, it is no wonder the human race has historically responded so wondrously to physical combat. It marries our hemispheres in art and brutality, geometry and instinct, function and hubris, imagination and satisfaction.

Rihn's self-imposed 100-word limit to his vignettes echoes the timed rounds and enforced limits of the matches they put to use. His prose poetry acknowledges the freedom *of* rules, instead of *from* them. It recalls Frost, and tennis without nets. His measurements are the comparative equalizers. In this examination of newness entering the world, of apocalypse, these astonishing disclosures, there *must* be an even distribution. What happens can only happen because of what preceded, can only determine what happens next.

Rihn is also a willing participant in his scrutiny. In considering the bested fighter on the canvas, he asks of himself as much as he asks of humanity: "What, then, do we say . . . [t]o the violence of such repose? . . . We breathe as if breath is silence. We watch as if witness is speech." This sentiment permeates existence. It shoulders action, inaction, what we celebrate, and what we castigate with worldly weight: the shapes of our lives, our communities.

Revelation taps an aspect of our nature that I find hard to put into words, and thus find confounding. I don't especially love boxing. I don't participate in the sport, nor do I make much of an effort to witness its performance. But when I hear people who do engage the sport talk about it, and I let my thoughts go where they will, I can't help but share in their romance. Witnessing the compelling can be a form of understanding. I can't quite explain why I'm so compelled to keep turning Rihn's pages, despite moments almost begging myself to stop in consideration of his theses, in appreciation of the beauty of his language. He's tapped into the desire to consume. At times, reading *Revelation* transforms me into the thirsty spectator, gladiators an arm's length away. I'm embracing the puns, words and lines landing, endings hitting hard, me on the ropes, clinching the pages, punch-drunk. At other times, I escape the basic wanting, awed by craft, by everywhere he invites my mind to wander.

Rihn doesn't answer the big questions he considers, and doesn't seek to. There isn't a big reveal, just the power to use what we can see to make sense of what we can't. We're all somewhere in the cycle, and we can't help but want to see what happens next, even when we think we already know.

Christopher Forrest
Press 53 Poetry Editor

How does newness come into the world? How is it born?

Of what fusions, translations, conjoinings is it made?

How does it survive, extreme and dangerous as it is? What compromises, what deals, what betrayals of its secret nature must it make to stave off the wrecking crew, the exterminating angel, the guillotine?

Salman Rushdie
The Satanic Verses

Revelation

Tyson vs. Mercedes

Mar 6, 1985

Plaza Convention Center, Albany, New York, U.S.

Mike Tyson comes into the ring already warmed up, already shadowboxing. The start of something: existential. But also, after the finish: history. Or also again: dramatic irony. The camera records, documents: produces records, documents. When Mike Tyson touches gloves, he nearly bows. The men are as tall as statues that have not yet been pulled down. Mercedes crumbles rather than falls, fading like a camera out of focus, blurred. Down on one knee, the fight is ended: this end is also a beginning. Something new has entered the world. Mike Tyson rushes over, palms up, as if almost to apologize.

Tyson vs. Singleton

Apr 10, 1985

Albany, New York, U.S.

Speak about violence. Or the violence that speaks *in* you and *through* you and *despite* you. The right hooks and the left. A moment later, Singleton drops to his knees. A moment we call *breath*; to relax, we say *breathe*. What, then, do we say to a fighter on the canvas? To the violence of such repose? Mike Tyson motions as if to throw another punch; a threat, a jeer, a throwback: Dempsey before the long count. We breathe as if breath is silence. We watch as if witness is speech. We hesitate to speak about violence. *Ite, missa est.*

Tyson vs. Halpin

May 23, 1985

Albany, New York, U.S.

There's the foreword, the precursor, the a priori from Lowell, Massachusetts, warming up, throwing punches in the air, good form, nondescript, like an extra from the set of a movie in which Mike Tyson is the star. He makes, we assume, what we have come to call a fearless moral inventory. Ron Howard was apprehensive about how to film the boxing sequences for *Cinderella Man*. Russell Crowe advised him: Shoot them like the fires in *Backdraft*. Mike Tyson celebrates like a bone before the break, careless synonyms of hand, stroke, and fist. Gloves like flames are raised above the ropes.

Tyson vs. Spain

Jun 20, 1985

Steel Pier, Atlantic City, New Jersey, U.S.

Mike Tyson's walk is a master class in slowness, his gloved hands hung low at his side, each step paced (i.e. *deliberate*) rather than pacing (i.e. *anxious*), so posed or poised, relaxed in appearance but brutal in context, almost plodding, step after conscious step, casual performance, neither excited nor winded. Character study. Count to ten (i.e. *breathe*). Spain on the canvas, amongst the ropes, exhales an exasperated *damn*. As if to say *to hell*, or from it. Madness as method, a lit fuse for a fist. The judgment, injury, examination. Heavy nights and pensive brows, like tarnished silver (i.e. *bruised*).

Tyson vs. Alderson

Jul 11, 1985

Trump Plaza Hotel and Casino, Atlantic City, New Jersey, U.S.

Avoid the *why*, begin with the *how*. Description before motivation. As messy as storytelling. Joyce Carol Oates will go on to call Mike Tyson *a savior, of sorts*, legendary *before there is a legend to define him*, while a D.C. newspaper, lamenting his purchase of a local house, will dismiss him in stark and cruel language: *Crazy or tortured, it doesn't much matter*. Alderson, a small cut blooming above his right eye, leans into the clinch, slowing Mike Tyson down, delaying the inevitable end, shortcoming. Years later, Mike Tyson will tell Matt Lauer: *If I'm drinking, I think about suicide.*

Tyson vs. Sims

Jul 19, 1985

Mid-Hudson Civic Center, Poughkeepsie, New York, U.S.

There is no footage of this fight. What is obvious: to call this a blackout. The nights no one remembers. *It's dangerous to hang out in this neighborhood alone*, says Mike Tyson, pointing to his own head. Remember. Those distant, misty nights. Those gray-faded memories like a melody that refuses to be hummed correctly. *It wants to kill everything,* says Mike Tyson. *It wants to kill me, too.* And so we listen, remember, humming along with the secrets and the rhythm. This is the covenant we make, the desert and the sea. This is the footage that makes everything possible.

Tyson vs. Canady

Aug 15, 1985

Steel Pier, Atlantic City, New Jersey, U.S.

Mike Tyson walks out wearing a cut-up sweatshirt draped over his shoulders, visceral aggression, unbound by convention, defying even basic fashion. *Mike reminds me of an oyster*, Sideeq, a spiritual advisor to Mike Tyson, will later comment. *An oyster has a very, very hard shell to protect a very, very soft inside.* After the fight, Mike Tyson speaks to the presenter. He makes eye contact and holds it with intention, as if they were completely alone. The words spill too quickly, the rehearsed speech of the timid, the introvert. This is the petition, the prayer. The unceasing famine, soft inside.

Tyson vs. Johnson

Sep 5, 1985

Atlantis Hotel and Casino, Atlantic City, New Jersey, U.S.

Twenty-four seconds into the fight, a left hook to the body drops Johnson, so immediate and clean one might think the fight was following a script. To watch is to wince; there is no passive viewership, no detached observation of these two men. Mike Tyson flows with the militancy of exorcism, addicted to that perfect chaos. The audience hesitates to cheer, afraid of taking sides against demon or priest. A right cross drops Johnson once more, responsorial hymn of calculated and deliberate ferocity. *Hitting a man*, writes J. R. Moehringer, *is sometimes the most satisfying response to being a man.*

Tyson vs. Long

Oct 9, 1985

Trump Plaza Hotel and Casino, Atlantic City, New Jersey, U.S.

Cus D'Amato once told Mike Tyson *I'm never going to work your corner, because if I die, I don't want you to look up and see my face missing.* Mike Tyson floors Long with a straight left to his face. A flurry drops him a second time. The ring is made up of empty spaces, like a memory, like a misunderstanding, interrupted by lavish, bruising contact. Long mouths *I'm ok* to the referee, Frank Capuccino, but soon is on the mat a third time, head between his gloves, face missing. The referee waves his arms through the empty space above.

Tyson vs. Colay

Oct 25, 1985

Atlantis Hotel and Casino, Atlantic City, New Jersey, U.S.

The ring announcer calls out Mike Tyson's name, explicit, enunciated, elongated. *Mike Tyyyy-son.* Then his last name repeated: *Tyy-son.* In the movie *Play It to the Bone*, Antonio Banderas plays an aging middleweight reliving a similar moment: *It was so cool just to hear your name so big.* Mike Tyson touches his gloves delicately to his own face, kissing them, extending open palms to the audience. His eyes widen a little, brows raise just a hair. The audience is hospitable, cheering. In the ring, Mike Tyson—his desolation momentarily rebuked—is welcomed by name. Synonyms for *welcome*: appreciated, longed-for, wanted.

Tyson vs. Benjamin

Nov 1, 1985

Coliseum, Latham, New York, U.S.

Mike Tyson slips Benjamin's jabs as crepuscular rays descend from overhead lights, as if the ring was lit by a cinematographer: a movie set. Belligerent and categorical stage direction. The crowd obscured in smoke, stale cigars, and the crowded space of sin. Darkness reminiscent of a George Bellows painting. The implicit cacophony of a sharp left hook. While Benjamin is counted out, Mike Tyson thrusts his gloved hands between the ropes, palms up. *(Like a small play,* to paraphrase Bruce Lee, *but played seriously.)* Pious objects and sacred signs. The expressive potential of the human figure. Tremble within: echo, resonate.

Tyson vs. Richardson

Nov 13, 1985

Ramada Hotel, Houston, Texas, U.S.

Correlation, this fight. The first right and the last left, residual, glimmering. *Tyson is a little icebox,* announces the sportscaster, *rather than a refrigerator.* As if metaphor could explain these brute poetics, as if these small fires could singe our wrists. The sportscaster asserts that Mike Tyson's neck is *approximately the same size of actress Shelley Duvall's waist.* As if this resolution would wash, as if these deluge waters could cover this seasoned ground. Imagine what flashed behind Richardson's eyes when he fell. Fast motion, popular apocalypse. What the architects said: *a building under assembly is a ruin in reverse.*

Tyson vs. Nelson

Nov 22, 1985

Coliseum, Latham, New York, U.S.

We learn about proportion. Fists, bodies, faces. The ring is tight, and the camera low. A cursory analysis strikes the chord of a cage, the blunt fact of separation. A syllabus for moving inside. Aggressive, and almost immediate. After the fight, two small boys run into the ring holding a sign proclaiming Mike Tyson "Doctor KO," troubler of the heavyweight division, prophet of forward motion, inevitability. The ring is teeming with debris and fate like a pedagogy, like a fist opening and closing. Tell me about it: the clutter. The tremor, the whisper, the word. Tell me about this stage.

Tyson vs. Scaff

Dec 6, 1985

Felt Forum, New York City, New York, U.S.

The ring is a desert on smelted pillars where the devil is both loosed and contained. There is blood on the glove. Mike Tyson, thunderous and poised in the ring, remembers that soon he will have to climb back down again. The mountains of the poets shake and tremble and melt; apocalyptic mountains are spread with flesh. Salt and sulfur and sins like mist. Reflections of demons, echoed voices ricocheting off the backs of teeth. Every demon was once an angel, after all. Blessed opponent, salvage. This is how we think of the descent. This is also how we climb.

Tyson vs. Young

Dec 27, 1985

Coliseum, Latham, New York, U.S.

Beautiful peacemaker, firebrand provocateur. Are you not a priest; why then do you stand in a cemetery? The right uppercut and Young's body flung into the ropes, facedown on the mat, being turned over by the ring doctor. Resonant phantasms, delirious and inchoate clues. *I expect them to be hungry, but I'm hungrier*, Mike Tyson says, in celebration and distress. Like Elijah, that lonely prophet from the Book of Kings, flood and fire sweeping this uncertain street. This earthly tempest, nauseating and claustrophobic. The ring is a halo, a speechless haven: a window into this good night, this satisfied kingdom.

Tyson vs. Jaco

Jan 11, 1986

Plaza Convention Center, Albany, New York, U.S.

There are things we cannot see. Imagine a tornado without debris: all cause and no effect. From certain angles, we cannot see Mike Tyson's fist, his uppercut—only the back of Jaco's rattled head, his snapping neck. We cannot see the sportscaster when he calls Mike Tyson a *human whirlwind*. Jaco, that spontaneous palooka, goes down three times, but doesn't believe it at first. This is how we walk by faith, shadowboxing the unseen. The way the human eye evolves. The substance, the presence, the appearance of things. This is how we learn to trust a transformation beyond our sight.

Tyson vs. Jameson

Jan 24, 1986

Trump Plaza Hotel and Casino, Atlantic City, New Jersey, U.S.

Quench the heart, liquid adrenaline and cold water from the river. On the cover of *Sports Illustrated*, Mike Tyson appears with the moniker "Kid Dynamite," blue shorts and smiling, the frightful stuff displaced like water from a bathtub. Inexplicably, the third round lasts only two minutes instead of the usual three. Human error, dedicated and vicious. After a knockdown, the referee asks Jameson if he is okay. Jameson's mouth says *yes*, but something else speaks to the ref—probably Jameson's eyes, red and losing focus—and he stops the fight. Claim all of this: the fuse, the detonation, the sensitivity.

Tyson vs. Ferguson

Feb 16, 1986

Houston Field House, Troy, New York, U.S.

Even halos can be square, if you know how to paint them. Martyrdom and grace and blood flowing from the broken nose of Ferguson. The corpus and the crux, two eyes on a golden plate. This bloodied aggregate implies there is more than mathematics would suggest. Consider those angles—how the triceps ("three-headed muscle of the arm") differs from the biceps ("two-headed muscle of the arm"). Consider the spear, the flame, the rope. What is meant by meat and what is meant by char. Frame of a painting, frame of a door. The squared circle, every corner of our day.

Tyson vs. Zouski

Mar 10, 1986

Nassau Veterans Memorial Coliseum, Uniondale, New York, U.S.

Every one is a grenade. Speed and shrapnel and the steady suddenness of explosion. Muhammad Ali was posed like a magazine saint: Saint Sebastian who, we forget, was actually healed of his arrows but later clubbed to death. (German monks preserved his cranium in silver, and drank wine from it to celebrate his feast day.) No one encouraged Mike Tyson to pretend to saintliness. "Kid Dynamite": this explosion posing as a man. The etymology of *explosion*: a clapping of hands, a rejection; as in the theater, to drive an actor off the stage. Bad seeds, this pomegranate, like sour fists.

Tyson vs. Tillis

May 3, 1986

Civic Center, Glens Falls, New York, U.S.

Mike Tyson reveals a head shaved to look like Jack Dempsey, no robe—all gladiator and walking mythos. Quick dominion suffocating this beautiful metaphor, this allegory of aggression. Tillis is nearly knocked out at the end of round one, *but*, as the *L.A. Times* comments philosophically, *what happened, happened.* This fight, Mike Tyson's twentieth, will be the first to go the distance, a revelation, a truth laid bare, which translates to *apocalypse*, once meaning *an insight* or even *a visionary hallucination.* Truncated and cut short, we now believe in the imminence of our own annihilation, *the end of the world.*

Tyson vs. Green

May 20, 1986

Madison Square Garden, New York City, New York, U.S.

New York, they said, was *busting out.* Iron and blood. Solid and liquid, like land and water: this island, this throwback. The new principles arrive, crown of ropes upon their heads, stone wings suspended along the rusty shorelines of their antiphons. O roots and keystones, prisoners of light and prisoners of darkness! O theory of constraint! Sit down and scrutinize this grief, this crisis in fact, disastrous metal and corrosion wrapped in fists. O punches thrown and punches landed, unanimous and opinionated! Come and shine upon the bare knuckles of this world. Bust this desolation, this cheap and fashionable dust.

Tyson vs. Gross

Jun 13, 1986

Madison Square Garden, New York City, New York, U.S.

Above the "Tale of the Tape" floats a small gold crown attached to a name in gold lettering: *DON*. The feigned divination of the TV guide. Pay per view. Prime time. The infinite ways we are distracted, seduced. The fight ends with a KO in the first round, perhaps the most beautiful twelve seconds of Mike Tyson's boxing career. Gross, who had been defending for the better part of the round, unloads a flurry of perhaps fifteen punches, all of which Mike Tyson successfully avoids before responding with a single left hook, flooring Gross. These replacement memories, ephemeral and prophetic.

Tyson vs. Hosea

Jun 28, 1986

Houston Field House, Troy, New York, U.S.

This is Mike Tyson's last fight as a teenager, a fight ended too soon, a path blocked with thornbushes. Hear this, you referees! You count the sand of the sea. Hear this, you judges and scorekeepers! You break the distance of blood, walking about the parched land of the ring apron. Hear this, you ring announcers, jeering fans, inchoate crowd awash in your emotion. Who is wise? Let them realize the righteous walk while the rebellious stumble. Let them seethe as bloodshed follows bloodshed. Do something about this, like people, like priests. Like muscles into meat, like fists into gloves.

Tyson vs. Boyd

Jul 11, 1986

Stevensville Hotel, Swan Lake, New York, U.S.

We note the fight's location, Swan Lake. The metaphors for good selves and bad. The camera focuses on Mike Tyson's right bicep, tattooed with the word *MIKE*, a small persistent thing he will later have covered up in prison. At twenty, Mike Tyson is already outgrowing the nickname *Kid Dynamite*, becoming *Iron*, becoming *the baddest man on the planet*. Boyd leans in low from the waist to avoid the hooks, but remains vulnerable to uppercuts. Mike Tyson's left hand is injured; Boyd's nose is broken. Vulnerable in his own raspy ways, Mike Tyson ends the fight without a cracking smile.

Tyson vs. Frazier
Jul 26, 1986

Civic Center, Glens Falls, New York, U.S.

There is, of course, the gritty specter of genealogy, the voices we think we hear, phantom limbs throwing their haunted punches. Clarified in the light of passion, rag doll, we dance and fall and crumble. Mysteries hidden within stones, their desolate weight, and the coldness of the universe within those black lights Muhammad Ali spoke about. Outward and visible, inward and obscured, our signs of grace, clinging and cleaved to with ropes and gloves, deathrock and horrorpunk, a body on the canvas, propped up by bones rather than by consciousness. Within this legacy of brutality, we count the visible synonyms.

Tyson vs. Ribalta

Aug 17, 1986

Trump Plaza Hotel and Casino, Atlantic City, New Jersey, U.S.

Here is the image, the cruciform optic. Above the "Tale of the Tape" are two photos: Ribalta posed smiling, shoulders angled, fists raised. And Mike Tyson, face square on, almost vacant in expression, like a mug shot. No more smiling in the ring, just a signifying gold tooth in the front line of a snarl. No more wide eyes, just an angry, furrowed brow. Elusive gladiator, antihero for the home box office. Pugilism wrapped in myth, fast on its way to an execution. Strange battle, new man: premonition of the fighter who doesn't fall, the stone we all have swallowed.

Tyson vs. Ratliff

Sep 6, 1986

Las Vegas Hilton, Winchester, Nevada, U.S.

Mike Tyson sits post-fight with a tuxedoed Sugar Ray Leonard, offering exposition: *Stay composed*, he advises. *Sometimes you get hit and you have to take it. Don't show no emotions.* The prophet Elijah once climbed a mountain, and by himself challenged eight hundred and fifty heathen priests. *I took it very personally when he called me a little kid.* In Las Vegas, there was no betting on a winner, only if the fight would end *before* the fifth round or *after*. Such tragic fires, the wreckage and futility that Mike Tyson faces. The assumption we knew what winning looked like.

Tyson vs. Berbick

Nov 22, 1986

Las Vegas Hilton, Winchester, Nevada, U.S.

What can be said: hydrogen bombs. God as a blessing in disguise, deadly and accurate. Moments of miracles and petulant left hooks. What Berbick said: *my life is the truth, and the truth is a mystery*. Revelation's funny punches: a jab like a good scream, what the *Daily Mail* called the *carnage below the chandeliers*. This is how newness enters the ring: cut-up towel over his shoulders, a modern Elijah proclaimed by acolytes, his sign lifted over their bowed heads. Crooked and enticing judgment day: our discernment is over, and only just beginning. Remember this new reign, its striking disclosure.

Tyson vs. Smith

Mar 7, 1987

Las Vegas Hilton, Winchester, Nevada, U.S.

Mike Tyson is not a ghost; he is the desolate wilderness, the new growth, recognizable in every place, not for dress or diet, but for doctrine and blood. For twelve rounds these men nullify expectations like shadow figures, trace elements. We hold on, endure, persisting in spite of our deductions. Afterwards, the sportscaster says the two men have released *the tension and hate* of their fight. Survival despite our dissections, our diversions, our thin attempts at definition. The bones we've crushed along the way and the broken efforts. A fist being raised, the adumbration of our best lives, the epiphany.

Tyson vs. Thomas

May 30, 1987

Las Vegas Hilton, Winchester, Nevada, U.S.

Imagine the rounds are stanzas, the fight a poem. Line breaks, enjambment, and rhythm. A torn glove on this hard road to glory. New and deadly dimensions, dramatic irony and alliteration. For example, Thomas sparred with a boxer nicknamed *Scrap Iron*. Refrain, repetition. Mike Tyson throws fewer punches in combination, those power punches, those hydrogen bombs. Synecdoche, epic, anaphora. Imagine the rounds are stanzas. Mike Tyson ends it in the sixth with a flurry of hooks, left and right. Blood from Thomas's lip drips down his chest. The real ferocity of a man in action, the poem and the page.

Tyson vs. Tucker

Aug 1, 1987

Las Vegas Hilton, Winchester, Nevada, U.S.

The final fight in the unification series—WBA, WBC, and IBF. Glory Hallelujah! and Tucker's robe made entirely of gold sequins. A coronation amidst a bald spot. Don King describing the *baubles, rubies and fabulous doodads*. This is the arid shrug of a fighter who climbed a mountain for God, and found only stone and sand; the roar and the cheer its own kind of silence, its own non-answer, agnostic in the face of revelation—that is to say, an abiding faith in bums instead of prophets. Mike Tyson's two fists and already the past tense, old testaments, wordless personae.

Tyson vs. Biggs

Oct 16, 1987

Convention Hall, Atlantic City, New Jersey, U.S.

Nintendo releases the game *Mike Tyson's Punch-Out!!* with two exclamation points built into the title, punctuation like twin fists, the scripture of their strike, solemn exposition of their brutal facts. Children can play along, controller in their hands like a finger on the pulse of American violence, avatar of adulthood and masculinity. Joyce Carol Oates observes that Mike Tyson's single-mindedness in the ring, his violence and wrath, have the quality of Old Testament justice: *his grievance has the force of a natural catastrophe*. At home, we learn to throw electronic punches against myth and man, pajamas and breakfast cereal, alone.

Tyson vs. Holmes
Jan 22, 1988

Convention Hall, Atlantic City, New Jersey, U.S.

The ring is a haunted world where rope separates limitless prophecy from constricting expectation. Mike Tyson can no longer hear the difference between *this is what is to come* and *this is all you ever can be*. Savage predictions, uncompromising. Call him a monster and you will find only a monster. Larry Holmes is knocked down three times in the fourth round, great crashing drops, the weight of history and canvas slicing instinct and shaky legs, painful applause. Mike Tyson, wallowing in the attention, rebukes context. Holmes after the fight: *They always get you and some day they'll get him.*

Tyson vs. Tubbs

Mar 21, 1988

Tokyo Dome, Tokyo, Japan

The Tokyo Dome is dubbed the *Big Egg* and the ring is full of gossip. Tubbs is overweight, people say. And Mike Tyson has married into the head of the class. *Sometimes*, Mike Tyson admits, *I feel like I left earth and went to another planet.* Don King, the people eater, businessman of the wasteland, weighs the profit of revelation, writing contracts like tragedies in which everyone dies. Tubbs displays admirable equanimity in the face of raw violence, but still, Mike Tyson's punches cut into the quick, and when Tubbs falls in the second, it is catachresis, terrible and lasting.

Tyson vs. Spinks

Jun 27, 1988

Convention Hall, Atlantic City, New Jersey, U.S.

Over in ninety-one seconds, and with only ten punches landed, this was supposed to be Mike Tyson's mountaintop, and perhaps it was, because who else can speak to the view from such heights? *I tried to take the shot and I came up short*, Spinks says after. Elijah was victorious on Mount Carmel, but anxious and alone, fled to Mount Horeb with all its wind and fire and earthquakes. And the mountain's disorientating sound of sheer silence. Mike Tyson becomes the lineal champion—the man who beat the man—to the sound of ambient noise and the clanking of chains.

Tyson vs. Bruno I

Feb 25, 1989

Las Vegas Hilton, Winchester, Nevada, U.S.

No longer an artist in the ring, Mike Tyson does not appear passionate either. Less footwork, less head movement, his elusiveness discarded. Wheedled down from complete man to character, experience down to performance, existence to persona. All the focus is on throwing power punches: heavy, wild knockout swings. Mike Tyson no longer fights with the nuanced authority of style (what boxers call *looking pretty* in the ring), instead dealing aggression in bulk order, measured out in tonnage, scorched-earth wholesale indiscriminate carpet-bombing, effective but blunt, more bulldozer than scalpel, more forest fire than blowtorch. We watch Mike Tyson burning himself out.

Tyson vs. Williams

Jul 21, 1989

Convention Hall, Atlantic City, New Jersey, U.S.

In the video game, we are promised a *dream fight* with Mike Tyson, a passage into logarithmic exhibition, crackling with syntactical and lexical ambiguity. Is the whole fight merely a dream? A fight within a dream? Or the fight as dream, as wish-fulfillment? We tear the heavens open, television's glass screen reflecting what happened when the truth went down onto the canvas, head snapping the bottom rope, eyes rolling back into the skull. Mike Tyson throws nothing but punches programmed with a wide margin for brutality. Pressboard proscenium for the home entertainment theater of blood, concussion dreams, childhood's 8-bit apologue.

Tyson vs. Douglas

Feb 11, 1990

Tokyo Dome, Tokyo, Japan

Before the fight, Mike Tyson stands in his corner, ancient, immobile, while Douglas bobs and hops and dances. Mike Tyson used to pounce after the bell, but now he hesitates. Douglas's jabs are fast and strong. Mountains and mouthpieces eventually flow down, trembled and murmuring. Even the oceans receive rebuke. *The only person who can beat Mike Tyson*, they say, *is Mike Tyson.* This is demolition by neglect. We yearn for the past and the meticulous absolution of the threshing sledge. Mike Tyson, lost in the tenth round, stumbling reminder that defeat itself is one way newness enters the world.

Tyson vs. Tillman

Jun 16, 1990

Caesars Palace, Paradise, Nevada, U.S.

The road back is paved with ghosts and specters, apparitions who evaporate like sweat in the warm Nevada night. Mike Tyson makes the sign of the cross standing on an advertisement for Diet Coke. The ring is staged outside, a temple apart, black sky dotted by stars and anxiety. *How much can you learn*, asks sportscaster Jim Lampley, *from two minutes and forty-seven seconds?* As if their made-for-TV specials weren't already outlining our demise, tabloid obituaries lowering the caskets of our inside stories. As if these ghosts wouldn't talk. *It's not the personal problems*, observes Mike Tyson. *It's the aftermath*.

Tyson vs. Stewart

Dec 8, 1990

Convention Hall, Atlantic City, New Jersey, U.S.

Mike Tyson's fists aim to understand rather than to be understood, and a short left hook drops Stewart in the first. The ring doctor checks his pupils for signs of brain damage while journalists cram cameras under the ropes, assembling something like perspective, the inevitable skew and circus. Lines between fact and fiction, myth and reality, are drawn and re-drawn as Nintendo drops Mike Tyson from the electronic world of *Punch-Out!!* as if some kind of natural order needed to be re-established. The *dream fight* was over, our televisions dark with misery and wonder. Empty hands shook like dead geraniums.

Tyson vs. Ruddock I

Mar 18, 1991

The Mirage, Paradise, Nevada, U.S.

How to trigger a riot: accept the penumbra of this fallen, fractured breath. Sketch those claustrophobic fears brawling in the blemished streets. Welcome the power and accuracy of the present, this subjective self, the ring now filled to the ropes with bodies, indistinguishable, ekphrastic. The referee admonishes all who will listen: *People must realize a man can surrender when he's on his feet*. Mike Tyson, whose violence is a one-man riot of form and void, who has already learned so much about suffering, about heartache and grief and mulish tenacity, has yet to realize the strength it takes to surrender.

Tyson vs. Ruddock II

Jun 28, 1991

The Mirage, Paradise, Nevada, U.S.

Proclaim your sestinas of rage and provocation, pronounce your haggard villanelles and brutal epistles. Bring your bitter judgment down from the summit, soured news and prosecution literature. Mike Tyson's descent was foretold by those who never wanted to see his ascent, who did not love the mountaintop, and consequently reject both the climber and the climb. Strike fast with the closed cinquain of your fist; the terza rima of these rounds will not last. The memory of this elegiac ring is cut from the earth, curses like oil seeping into the bones. Afflicted heart, why should you be beaten anymore?

Tyson vs. McNeeley

Aug 19, 1995

MGM Grand Garden Arena, Paradise, Nevada, U.S.

We wonder about rehabilitation, reform, redemption: the enthusiasm of Elijah, after his mountain expeditions, consuming soldier after soldier in Godly fire. McNeeley, for all his sacrifice and futile bravery, promises to wrap Mike Tyson in a *cocoon of horror*. But a right hook floors him in the first ten seconds. And then an uppercut drops him a second time. At 1:29 into the first round, his corner throws in the towel. This conclusion was foregone; the spectacle, monstrous. Teddy Atlas, shrewd as thorns, explains the cynicism: fights like this exist only to exploit people's willingness *to believe in this monster*.

Tyson vs. Mathis Jr.

Dec 16, 1995

CoreStates Spectrum, Philadelphia, Pennsylvania, U.S.

Mike Tyson talks Moses and gladiators: *The nightmares of thousands of generations live on in the heads of the living.* They bill this fight "Presumption of Innocence," without apology or explanation. Mike Tyson's aim is not what it once was; Mathis slips punches until a combination in the third drops him to the canvas. When Mike Tyson was dropped from the electronic world of *Punch-Out!!*, his character wasn't deleted, but converted into *Mr. Dream*. Designers changed the head and skin color but kept the body the same: ephemeral daydream, sprite of the unreal, foil to the nightmare we already knew.

Tyson vs. Bruno II

Mar 16, 1996

MGM Grand Garden Arena, Paradise, Nevada, U.S.

Life within the law, says Don King, *is where the real villains are*, the sunset within his scheming eyes drowned in blood-red brine. Body shots to Bruno's torso translate like flowers of evil, evening harmonies to thrill a tortured heart. Melancholy waltz! Languid vertigo! We witness what one scholar callously designated *the fragmentation of Mike Tyson*. The skies like a mosque are beautiful and stern, and the fight is the fight between silence and cacophony, affirming the hope that good deeds might indeed erase the bad. *You'll find*, says Bruno, *that I was a little brokenhearted when it was over*.

Tyson vs. Seldon

Sep 7, 1996

MGM Grand Garden Arena, Paradise, Nevada, U.S.

To indicate the kind of death that shadowboxes within these human allusions, the symbolic death of the KO, the count to ten, and that amenable slip into unconsciousness, Mike Tyson describes assassins who kill people, but other kinds of assassins as well: *Guys that lurk behind school buses and wait for you to fall in the snow.* Tupac Shakur, if he ever really died, is murdered after this fight, as if this death could be a kind of liberation. He raps: *All they see is black venom, then my silhouette.* Wake up the dead. There is work to be done.

Tyson vs. Holyfield I

Nov 9, 1996

MGM Grand Garden Arena, Paradise, Nevada, U.S.

Finally, Giant Killer, the confession of fate's delay. What does it mean to show your pain to 16,000 people? Giant Killer, what does it mean to punish a man who rubs his head on the earth? Richard Hoffer describes Mike Tyson's *desire to hurt* without clarification: a desire *to inflict hurt*, or *to be hurt* himself? Remnants of the dream fight tear the flesh above Mike Tyson's eye. The ring is a broken cosmos beyond speculation or hypothesis, Giant Killer, unraveling with every word. *Any more punishment,* says referee Mitch Halpern after stopping the fight, *would have been too much.*

Tyson vs. Holyfield II

Jun 28, 1997

MGM Grand Garden Arena, Paradise, Nevada, U.S.

The day before the fight, Mike Tyson laid a wreath on Sonny Liston's grave, special enforcer of this sound and this fury. As a young savage in the ring, Mike Tyson was an earth-shaking prophet of fire. Now our aging Elijah visits Ahab the king in his vineyard: stolen land, injustice and retribution. Poor maneuvering souls, they walk upon a ring of gold and crowns. Mike Tyson starts the third round without his mouth guard, the fight hanging loose like vestigial flesh. *I still love Mike*, says Holyfield. *It's just those demons that possess him and make him do things.*

Tyson vs. Botha

Jan 16, 1999

MGM Grand Garden Arena, Paradise, Nevada, U.S.

The aesthetic of the rejected, the forbidden, discarded. As if left to die by somber stereotype and the scattering of dried leaves. Be real: it's dark and Hell is hot. Mike Tyson is not simply replaced by Mr. Dream, but haunted, cursed. The same moves, and yet not the same: doppelganger, body double, unwanted twin. Grab the arm and twist, try to break it. Clinch after the bell, swing and push. Still, Mike Tyson's aggression fades by the fourth round. When Botha feints, Mike Tyson flinches. Unspoken, the wicked and the flame like a leaping trestle, all quiver and rust.

Tyson vs. Norris

Oct 23, 1999

MGM Grand Garden Arena, Paradise, Nevada, U.S.

In the ring, Mike Tyson can face his demons but he cannot relinquish them. It is true that he can fight and it is true that he can win, yet he cannot carry that victory out with him, cannot keep hold of it. Those demons follow him through the ropes, into the hostile neon exposure. What partnership has righteousness with lawlessness? What fellowship has light with darkness? Mike Tyson, who was once superior to the rules of the fight, is now awash in a tide pool of resentments, flushing in detritus and rinsing out the silky flotsam of disrobed anguish.

Tyson vs. Francis

Jan 29, 2000

MEN Arena, Manchester, England

No prophet is accepted in his own country. Mike Tyson takes refuge inside a Brixton police station, a familiar ring in a foreign land, and asks by bullhorn to be broken out. A British newspaper bought advertising space on the soles of Francis's shoes, anticipating the front page photos of him laid low, their logo foreshortened in dramatic fashion. And yet, Mike Tyson looks to the referee, his eyes asking for a break to every clinch, an opportunity to set up his power punches—opportunities he once would have opened himself. These longshot days without sympathy, grim and fugitive, desiccating.

Tyson vs. Savarese

Jun 24, 2000

Hampden Park, Glasgow, Scotland

The ring like a scroll, a monologue, a place where prophecy can reveal newness shimmering like a bruise on the flesh of the world. *One thing about Tyson that you can be sure of*, writes James Mossop, *is that he senses the finish is imminent and knows how to execute it*. The river's cool waters parted by a rolled-up robe. The cloth we are cut from, the teardrops and the dew. A *finish* and not an *end*; an *execution* and not a *performance*. The carnage of flesh like a holy recitation whispered from the ring, the inscrutable remains, never finished.

Tyson vs. Golota

Oct 20, 2000

The Palace, Auburn Hills, Michigan, U.S.

Golota, known for fighting dirty and throwing low blows, stands toe-to-toe with Mike Tyson: two bad men, guillotines of our collective conscience, breaking bones for us. The desolate flock weeps and howls like a new moon turned to blood, devouring their popcorn decay. If Mike Tyson is in fact Mike Tyson's own worst enemy, he is not only Elijah but also Ahab, both the fiery prophet and the scoundrel king. Golota quits the fight after two rounds, shoving his cornerman, pushing the referee. Mike Tyson stands on the ropes, an attempted celebration, tiny nation bounded by a chorus of jeers.

Tyson vs. Nielsen

Oct 13, 2001

Parken Stadium, Copenhagen, Denmark

What doppelganger voice calls to Mike Tyson, urging him to open that desperate crown of attrition? The righteous path is level, but in this ring, Mike Tyson still can stumble. Mr. Dream lingers like an image, spitting: like a low blow. But whose dream was he? From what collective unconscious did he grow? After a low blow, the injured fighter is allowed up to five minutes to recover, and if he cannot recover, is considered to be knocked out. The biology of a human skeleton, unforgiving, unpredictable. Mike Tyson stands haunted, occupied, every bad dream recurring like a ruthless sunrise.

Tyson vs. Lewis

Jun 8, 2002

The Pyramid, Memphis, Tennessee, U.S.

One last dream fight, last promise within demolished arguments and captive thoughts. Before the fight, security officers cut a yellow line of bodies diagonally through the ring, protecting the fighters from themselves. Without taking sides, boxing columnist Thomas Hauser forwards the debate *as to whether Tyson has suffered more at the hands of society than society has suffered at the hands of Tyson*. Lewis fights on the outside, all footwork and stiff jabs. Blood drips around Mike Tyson's eyes, falling onto the ring. Real strength shows most effectively from within our weakness. Where will we be when history goes down?

Tyson vs. Etienne

Feb 22, 2003

The Pyramid, Memphis, Tennessee, U.S.

A crushed spirit dries up the bones of philosophy, reduces humanity to little more than theory, unsound and sordid calculation murmuring: *Tyson's life can never point to anything larger than itself: his own self-serving actions, his own madness, his own befuddlement and consternation before the revelation of his limitations.* Such is the ceaseless prison. A prophet does not speak to hear his own voice any more than a boxer punches to feel himself sweat. Critics see only the fight between two boxers, but the fight was always larger than that. The real fight was always Mike Tyson versus the world.

Tyson vs. Williams

Jul 30, 2004

Freedom Hall, Louisville, Kentucky, U.S.

We keep watching, waiting for Mike Tyson to separate from these brutal techniques, from the pattern of this world: an ascension into the whirlwind. The fighter refuses death, and in doing so, also rejects the possibility of resurrection. Statues of saints are known to weep tears of blood in times of great stress. Mike Tyson, rattling like a bridge between opposing stockades, suggesting a kind of salvation for us all, reminds us that *what is reckless on the stage is splendor in the ring*. This man of hearts, not alone, alone: Cus D'Amato's face still missing from Mike Tyson's corner.

Tyson vs. McBride

Jun 11, 2005

MCI Center, Washington, D.C., U.S.

In the demon-haunted ring, Mike Tyson punches the heavy bags of ghosts, recurring like nightmares, tragedy born without gloves, the bare-fisted brute poetics of a screaming heart, headbutts and uppercuts, bloody-mouthed and swollen. When one declares *it's me against the world* and wins, when the world has been bested, the fighter stands alone: worldless, homeless, destitute. A priest without a parish, prophet without a revelation. A staggering silence remains long after the mountaintop crumbles. Mike Tyson, this modern Elijah: the fighter, the son, the husband, the father, prophetic and frail human being, quits on his stool, waiting to be reborn.

Notes

Tyson vs. Singleton, pg. 4

Dempsey before the long count
A controversy from the 1927 Dempsey vs. Tunney fight

Ite, missa est
Latin phrase ("Go, it is dismissed"), formerly used to end the Catholic Mass

Tyson vs. Halpin, pg. 5

Shoot them like the fires in Backdraft
Described by Ron Howard on the director's commentary track of *Backdraft*

Tyson vs. Alderson, pg. 7

a savior, of sorts
On Boxing, Joyce Carol Oates, 1987

before there is a legend to define him
ibid.

Crazy or tortured, it doesn't much matter
"Neighborhood Bully," Jack Tapper, *Washington City Paper*, December 11, 1998

If I'm drinking, I think about suicide
From an August 29, 2013 interview, though I first saw this quote referenced in Michael Rappaport's 2017 book *This Book Has Balls*

Notes

Tyson vs. Sims, pg. 8

It's dangerous to hang out in this neighborhood alone
"Mike Tyson: 'I Did A Lot of Bad Things, and I Want to Be Forgiven,'" Austin Knoblauch, *L. A. Times,* August 24, 2013

It wants to kill everything. It wants to kill me, too
ibid.

Tyson vs. Canady, pg. 9

Mike reminds me of an oyster
"Neighborhood Bully," Jack Tapper, *Washington City Paper,* December 11, 1998

Tyson vs. Johnson, pg. 10

perfect chaos
Mike Tyson quoted from a 2010 article in *Details* magazine

Hitting a man is sometimes the most satisfying response to being a man
"Resurrecting the Champ," J. R. Moehringer, *L. A. Times,* May 4, 1997. Also the basis for a mostly-forgotten movie of the same name starring Samuel L. Jackson and Josh Hartnett

Tyson vs. Long, pg. 11

I'm never going to work your corner
"A Force Unleashed," Tim Layden, *Sports Illustrated,* March 6, 1985

Notes

Tyson vs. Colay, pg. 12

It was so cool just to hear your name so big
Play It to the Bone, 1999

Tyson vs. Benjamin, pg. 13

Like a small play, but played seriously
Enter the Dragon, 1973

Tyson vs. Richardson, pg. 14

a building under assembly is a ruin in reverse
Alison and Peter Smithson, English architects associated with New Brutalism

Tyson vs. Nelson, pg. 15

Doctor KO
Reference to pitcher Dwight Gooden's nickname "Doctor K"

troubler of the heavyweight division
Reference to 1 Kings 18:17

Tyson vs. Scaff, pg. 16

The mountains of the poets
Dictionary of Biblical Imagery, Leland Ryken, 1998

spread with flesh
Ezekiel 32:5

Notes

Tyson vs. Young, pg. 17

Are you not a priest; why then do you stand in a cemetery?
Babylonian Talmud, Baba Mezi'a 114b

I expect them to be hungry, but I'm hungrier
Quoted on *BoxRec.com* for Tyson vs. Young

this good night
"Do Not Go Gently into that Good Night," Dylan Thomas

this satisfied kingdom
Dictionary of Biblical Imagery, Leland Ryken, 1998

Tyson vs. Jaco, pg. 18

spontaneous palooka
From the title of Jaco's 2012 autobiography

we walk by faith
2 Corinthians 5:7

the substance, the presence
Catholics believe in the "substantial presence" of Christ in the Eucharist

Tyson vs. Jameson, pg. 19

liquid adrenaline
Epinephrine, used by cutmen to stop bleeding between rounds, described in detail by F. X. Toole, see "The Monkey Look"

the cover of Sports Illustrated
January 1986

frightful stuff
Erroneous YouTube closed caption of commentator

Notes

Tyson vs. Ferguson, pg. 20

halos can be square
Common practice in religious paintings; square halos often denote living subjects

two eyes on a golden plate
Saint and martyr Lucy is often depicted this way

every corner of our day
From a prayer to St. Lucy

Tyson vs. Zouski, pg. 21

posed like a magazine saint
Cover of *Esquire*, April 1968

Tyson vs. Tillis, pg. 22

what happened, happened
"Tyson Wins But Not by a Knockout: Decision over Tillis Snaps Streak by Young Heavyweight," Richard Hoffer, *L. A. Times*, May 4, 1986

Tyson vs. Green, pg. 23

busting out
Fight billed as "New York Is Busting Out"

Iron and blood
Nicknames: "Iron" Mike Tyson and Mitch "Blood" Green

new principles
Erroneous YouTube closed caption of ring announcer

theory of constraint
"Boxing: The Sweet Science of Constraints," Joseph Lewandowski, *Journal of the Philosophy of Sport*, 2007

Notes

Tyson vs. Gross, pg. 24

DON
Reference to Don King

Tyson vs. Hosea, pg. 25

path blocked with thornbushes
Hosea 2:6

Hear this
Hosea 5:1

parched land
Hosea 2:3

Who is wise?
Hosea 14:9

Tyson vs. Frazier, pg. 27

genealogy
Marvis Frazier is the son of heavyweight champion Joe Frazier

those black lights
Quote widely attributed to Muhammad Ali, made especially famous as the epigraph (and title) to Thomas Hauser's 1985 book *The Black Lights: Inside the World of Professional Boxing*

Outward and visible, inward and obscured
St. Augustine of Hippo defines Catholic sacraments as "an outward and visible sign of an inward and invisible grace"

deathrock and horrorpunk
Musical subgenres

legacy of brutality
1985 album from the Misfits, an example of horrorpunk

Notes

Tyson vs. Ribalta, pg. 28

Strange battle, new man
A sort of portmanteau of officials' names: Judge Richard Strange, Referee Rudy Battle, and Judge Phil Newman

Tyson vs. Ratliff, pg. 29

Stay composed
Mike Tyson speaking to Sugar Ray Leonard after the fight

eight hundred and fifty heathen priests
1 Kings 18:19

I took it very personally when he called me a little kid
"Tyson stops Ratliff, looks to Berbick," *Observer-Reporter*, September 7, 1986

Tyson vs. Berbick, pg. 30

hydrogen bombs
"Tyson Knocks Out Berbick in Second to Earn WBC Title," Richard Hoffer, *L. A. Times*, November 23, 1986

deadly and accurate and *funny punches*
"Mike Tyson-Trevor Berbick: 30 years Later," Lee Groves, *The Ring*, 2016

my life is the truth, and the truth is a mystery
"Getting a Belt Out of Life," Pat Putnam, *Sports Illustrated*, December 1, 1986

carnage below the chandeliers
"Mike Tyson shook the world by beating Trevor Berbick... 30 years to the day since he became the youngest heavyweight champion in history," Jeff Powell, *Daily Mail*, November 21, 2016

judgment day
Fight billed as "Judgment Day"

Notes

Tyson vs. Smith, pg. 31

recognizable in every place
"The Church is recognizable in every place, not because of a common language or special dress or diet, but because of its doctrine and worship," *The Creed*, Scott Hahn, 2016

The bones we've crushed
Smith's nickname was "Bonecrusher"

Tyson vs Thomas, pg. 32

hard road
Fight billed as "Hard Road to Glory"

Tyson vs. Tucker, pg. 33

WBA, WBC, IBF
World Boxing Association, World Boxing Council, International Boxing Federation

Glory Hallelujah!
Phrase included on the fight's advertising

baubles, rubies and fabulous doodads
"Only One No. 1," Pat Putnam, *Sports Illustrated*, August 10, 1987

bums
"Thity years after Mike Tyson become champion, unfulfilled promise is the lasting memory" Wallace Matthews, *The Washington Post*, November 21, 2016

Tyson vs. Biggs, pg. 34

his grievance has the force of a natural catastrophe
On Boxing, Joyce Carol Oates, 1987

Notes

Tyson vs. Holmes, pg. 35

They always get you and some day they'll get him
"Tyson Keeps Title With 3 Knockdowns in Fourth," Phil Berger
New York Times, January 23, 1988

Tyson vs. Tubbs, pg. 36

head of the class
Reference to Robin Givens, the actress Mike Tyson married, who starred on the show *Head of the Class*

Sometimes I feel like I left earth and went to another planet
Quoted on *BoxRec.com* for Tyson vs. Tubbs

the people eater, businessman of the wasteland
"The People Eater" is a character in *Mad Max: Fury Road*, described on the Mad Max Fandom Wiki as "a degenerate businessman of the Wasteland"

Tyson vs. Spinks, pg. 37

I tried to take the shot and I came up short
"Spinks Didn't Fight According to Plan," Dave Anderson, *New York Times*, June 28, 1988

fled to Mount Horeb
1 Kings 19:8-12

the sound of ambient noise and the clanking of chains
"The man behind the most intimidating boxing walk-out music of all time," Pierre Richardson, *On The A Side*, January 26, 2016

Notes

Tyson vs. Bruno I, pg. 38

an artist in the ring, Mike Tyson does not appear passionate either
Reference to "'boxing' is an art, but 'fighting' is the passion."
On Boxing, Joyce Carol Oates, 1987

Tyson vs. Williams, pg. 39

We tear the heavens open
Isaiah 64:1

a wide margin for brutality
"Tyson Stuns Williams with Knockout in 1:33," Phil Berger, *New York Times,* July 22, 1989

Tyson vs. Douglas, pg. 40

Mountains and mouthpieces eventually flow down
Isaiah 64:1

Even the oceans receive rebuke
Psalms 18:15

The only person who can beat Mike Tyson is Mike Tyson
Sportscaster for Tyson vs. Berbick

This is demolition by neglect
"A situation in which a property owner intentionally allows a historic property to suffer severe deterioration, potentially beyond the point of repair," National Trust for Historic Preservation

threshing sledge
Isaiah 41:15

Tyson vs. Tillman, pg. 41

The road back
Fight billed as "The Road Back"

Notes

How much can you learn from two minutes
Jim Lampley speaking to Mike Tyson post-fight

tabloid obituaries lowering the caskets of our inside stories.
Fire and Fear: The Inside Story of Mike Tyson, Jose Torres, 1989

It's not the personal problems. It's the aftermath
Post-fight interview with Jim Lampley and Sugar Ray Leonard

a temple apart
1 Kings 9:3

Tyson vs Stewart, pg. 42

to understand, rather than to be understood
"The Prayer of St. Francis"—also included in the hymn "Make Me a Channel of Your Peace"

misery and wonder
Drew Bundini Brown quoted in *The Fight*, Norman Mailer, 1975

dead geraniums
"Rhapsody on a Windy Night," T.S. Eliot

Tyson vs. Ruddock I, pg. 43

power and accuracy
Quote from fight commentator

People must realize a man can surrender when he's on his feet
"A Controversy: Tyson Wins in 7th Round: Boxing: Referee Steele again in the middle, deciding that Ruddock is unable to continue. A brawl ensues," Earl Gustkey, *L. A. Times*, March 19, 1991

form and void
Genesis 1:2. Also used as the title for the final episode of *True Detective* Season 1

Tyson vs. Ruddock II, pg. 44

curses like oil seeping into the bones
Psalm 109:18

Afflicted heart, why should you be beaten anymore?
Isaiah 1:5

Tyson vs. McNeeley, pg. 45

consuming soldier after soldier in Godly fire
2 Kings 1:10

cocoon of horror
"The Big Question," Richard Hoffer, *Sports Illustrated*, August 21, 1995

to believe in this monster
ibid.

Tyson vs. Mathis Jr., pg. 46

The nightmares of thousands of generations
"Mike Tyson, History Buff," Amy Nicholson, *Village Voice*, March 11, 2015

Tyson vs. Bruno II, pg. 47

Life within the law is where the real villains are
The Black Lights: Inside the World of Professional Boxing, Thomas Hauser, 1985

drowned in blood-red brine
From various translations of Charles Baudelaire's poem "Evening Harmony," archived at https://fleursdumal.org/

Notes

evening harmonies to thrill a tortured heart
ibid.

Melancholy waltz! Languid vertigo!
ibid.

the fragmentation of Mike Tyson
Tyson: Nurture of the Beast, Ellis Cashmore, 2005

The skies like a mosque
From various translations of Charles Baudelaire's poem "Evening Harmony," archived at https://fleursdumal.org/

that good deeds might indeed erase the bad
Quran 11:114

You'll find that I was a little brokenhearted when it was over
"Boxing: Tyson Reclaims His First Championship Belt," Gerald Eskenazi, *New York Times*, March 17, 1996

Tyson vs. Seldon, pg. 48

To indicate the kind of death
John 12:33

Guys that lurk behind school buses and wait for you to fall in the snow.
"Tyson on Edge as Fight Starts," Greg Logan, *Altoona Mirror*, August 17, 1995

all they see is black venom, then my silhouette
"Letz Get It On (Ready 2 Rumble)," Tupac Shakur. Walkout music recorded specifically for this fight

Tyson vs. Holyfield I, pg. 49

Giant Killer
"Real Deal," Richard Hoffer, *Sports Illustrated*, November 1996

desire to hurt
ibid.

Any more punishment would have been too much
"Requiem for a Referee; Tears & Respect for Tragic Referee," Wallace Matthews, *NY Post*, August 23, 2000

Tyson vs. Holyfield II, pg. 50

laid a wreath on Sonny Liston's grave
"Fear and Clothing in Las Vegas," Rick Reilly, *Sports Illustrated*, July 7, 1997

special enforcer
Mike Tyson was named "special enforcer" for WWE's Wrestlemania XIV

this sound and this fury
Fight billed as "The Sound and The Fury"

Ahab the king in his vineyard
1 Kings 21

I still love Mike; it's just those demons that possess him and make him do things
"Feeding Frenzy: A Raging Mike Tyson Dragged His Sport to New Depths When He Sank His Teeth into Evander Holyfield," Richard Hoffer, *Sports Illustrated*, July 7, 1997

Notes

Tyson vs. Botha, pg. 51

Be real
Slogan printed on sweatshirts worn by Mike Tyson in the 1990s

it's dark and Hell is hot
DMX album title, 1998. Mike Tyson used "Intro" for walkout music

Tyson vs. Norris, pg. 52

What partnership has righteousness with lawlessness? What fellowship has light with darkness?
2 Corinthians 6:14

Tyson vs. Francis, pg. 53

No prophet is accepted
Luke 4:24

Tyson vs. Savarese, pg. 54

a monologue
This fight is notable for Mike Tyson's post-fight monologue

One thing about Tyson that you can be sure of
"Boxing: Referee hit in Tyson's 38 seconds of farce," James Mossop, *The Telegraph*, June 25, 2000

a rolled-up robe
2 Kings 2:8

Notes

Tyson vs. Golota, pg. 55

flock weeps and howls
Jeremiah 25:34

a new moon turned to blood
There are multiple references to this in the Bible; see for instance Revelation 6:12

Tyson vs. Nielsen, pg. 56

The righteous path
Isaiah 26:7

Tyson vs. Lewis, pg. 57

demolished arguments and captive thoughts
2 Corinthians 10:5

Real strength shows most effectively from within our weakness
2 Corinthians 12:9-10

when history goes down
Advertised on the fight poster: "Where will you be when history goes down?"

Tyson vs. Etienne, pg. 58

crushed spirit dries up the bones
Proverbs 17:22

Tyson's life can never point to anything larger than itself
"Mike's Brilliant Career: Mike Tyson and the Riddle of Black Cool," Gerald Early, *Transition*, 71, 1996

Notes

Tyson vs. Williams, pg. 59

from the pattern of this world
Romans 12:2

an ascension into the whirlwind
2 Kings 2

what is reckless on the stage is splendor in the ring
"TCA: Spike Lee Calls His 'Mike Tyson: Undisputed Truth' Subject 'The Most Honest Human Being I've Met in My Life,'" Alison Willmore, *IndieWire*, July 25, 2013

Andrew Rihn is the author of numerous scholarly articles and chapbooks of poetry, including *America Plops and Fizzes* (sunnyoutside press, 2010) and *Song of the Rescue* (EMP Books, 2019). He writes a boxing column, The Pugilist, for *Into the Void* magazine. He was born in Canton, Ohio, where he still lives.

www.ingramcontent.com/pod-product-compliance
Lightning Source LLC
LaVergne TN
LVHW041342080426
835512LV00006B/582